LIGHTNING BOLT BOOKS™

T0351850

Robots on the Job

Lola Schaefer

Lerner Publications • Minneapolis

Thank you, Jeff Rosen, Program Director—Engineering, Robotics, and Advanced Technologies at Georgia Institute of Technology, for your careful assistance with this book.

Lerner Publications Company
An imprint of Lerner Publishing Group, Inc.
241 First Avenue North
Minneapolis, MN 55401 USA

For reading levels and more information, look up this title at www.lernerbooks.com.

Main body text set in Billy Infant regular.
Typeface provided by SparkType.

Editor: Rebecca Higgins: **Photo Editor:** Cynthia Zemlicka

Library of Congress Cataloging-in-Publication Data

Names: Schaefer, Lola M., 1950- author.
Title: Robots on the job / Lola Schaefer.
Description: Minneapolis : Lerner Publications, [2021] | Series: Lightning bolt books. Robotics | Includes bibliographical references and index. | Audience: Ages 6-9. | Audience: Grades 2-3. | Summary: "Imagine a robot mowing your yard or performing surgery on you. In the future, they just might! Readers will discover how robots will help police, save lives, and more"— Provided by publisher.
Identifiers: LCCN 2019055106 (print) | LCCN 2019055107 (ebook) | ISBN 9781541596986 (library binding) | ISBN 9781728413600 (paperback) | ISBN 9781728400457 (ebook)
Subjects: LCSH: Robots—Juvenile literature.
Classification: LCC TJ211.2 .S332 2021 (print) | LCC TJ211.2 (ebook) | DDC 629.8/92—dc23

LC record available at https://lccn.loc.gov/2019055106
LC ebook record available at https://lccn.loc.gov/2019055107

Manufactured in the United States of America
1-47804-48244-2/21/2020

Table of Contents

Robots Can Do It!

Do you need to wash two hundred dishes? A robot can do it! Do you need your dog walked? A robot can do it! Robots can work a lot and never get tired.

A robot follows instructions called programs to complete a job. Robots make fewer mistakes than humans do.

An engineer uses a computer to program a robot.

This robot can lift a car.

Robots can lift heavy things over and over again! Some robots are stronger than any person is.

A robot can do things that are difficult for people to do. A robot can map the jungle or take video of the desert. Robots can work for days without needing a break.

Flying robots can explore places that are hard to get to.

On the Move

A robot's sensors help it move while it works. Sensors note and record the shapes, sounds, and size of items near the robot.

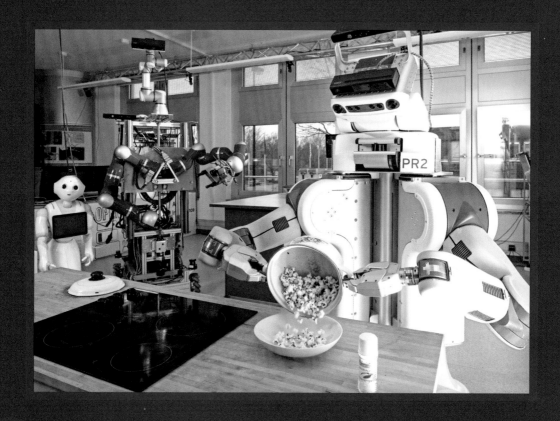

Many robots move to do their job. Some robots walk with feet. Others roll on wheels. Tracks help robots travel across grass, dirt, sand, or rock.

This robots rolls on its wheels to deliver groceries.

An engineer tells a robot where to cut.

Some robots are steered by an engineer. The engineer sends signals to the robot's computer that tells it what to do. Other robots are programmed to move by themselves.

Many robots have arms. The arms can be long or short. They may bend in many places. The arms have handlike parts that can grab, hold, or lift items.

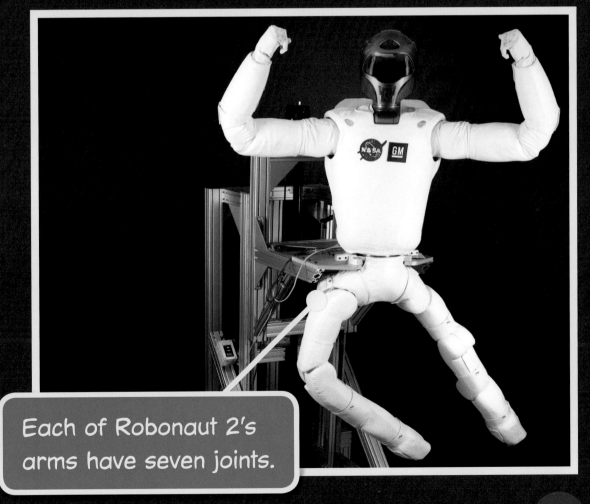

Each of Robonaut 2's arms have seven joints.

Robots at Home

You might have a robot working in your home. Small robot vacuums roll across floors. Their brushes pick up dirt and lint.

Robots babysit children. They play games with them on built-in screens. They help with homework. These robots are small so children can speak to them face-to-face.

Some robot babysitters have apps to entertain kids.

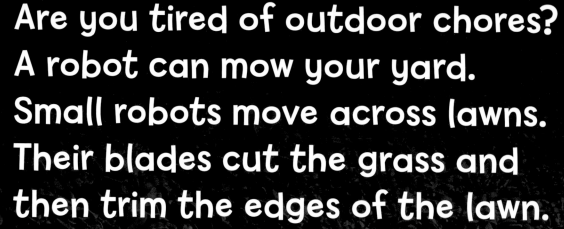

Are you tired of outdoor chores?
A robot can mow your yard.
Small robots move across lawns.
Their blades cut the grass and
then trim the edges of the lawn.

Some mowing robots
are quiet enough to
work day or night.

This robot patrols schools, malls, and more.

Some robots patrol homes. Their sensors notice any new sounds, smells, or people. If the robots sense danger, they send messages to their owners' cell phones.

Hard at Work

If you walk into a business, a robot might greet you. The robot can give directions and answer questions.

These robots work together to build cars.

Many factories use robots. These machines can work twenty-four hours a day. They can repeat the same task again and again.

Robots map the surface of moons and planets. They collect rocks and dirt. They also take photographs and video. The robots send the information back to people on Earth.

This robot maps Mars and sends data to scientists.

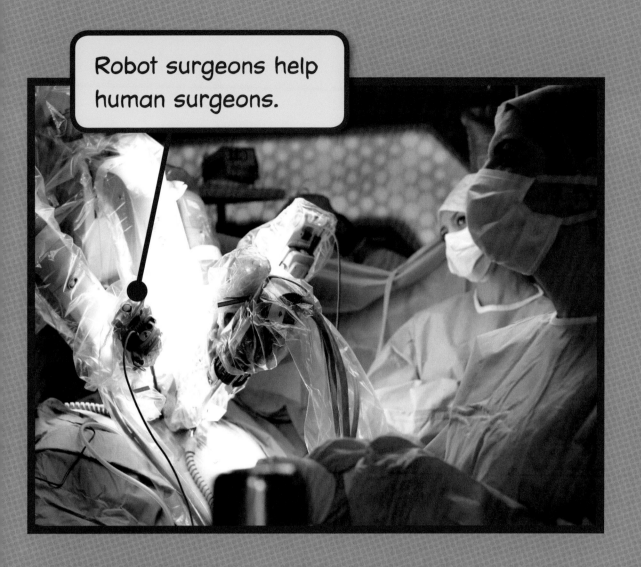

Robot surgeons help human surgeons.

Hospitals use robots to perform some surgeries. The robot arm stays steady for hours. It makes small cuts so patients recover more quickly.

Behind the Robot

You don't have to wait to work with robots. You can start now! Join a robotics team, and learn how to design and program a robot that will compete against other robots. You can continue on teams through high school. Degrees and jobs are also available in robotics.

Fun Facts

- Robot dogs and cats are popular. They don't shed hair. They don't bite. And they don't need to go to the bathroom.

- Doctors and scientists are working together to create nanobots. These tiny robots will enter human bodies and fight diseases.

- Police use robots to defuse bombs. It's safer for a robot to do it.

Glossary

engineer: someone who is trained to design and build machines

factory: a building where products, such as cars or shoes, are made

patrol: to walk or travel around an area to protect it

program: instructions for a computer or robot to follow

sensor: a device that can notice and record heat, size, shape, sound, or pressure

surface: the outside or outermost layer of something

surgery: an operation to repair, remove, or replace injured or diseased parts of the body

tracks: endless belts on which a vehicle travels

Further Reading

CBC Kids
https://www.cbc.ca/kidscbc2/the-feed/robots
-rule-this-restaurant

Colins, Luke. *Animal Robots*. Mankato, MN: Black
Rabbit Books, 2020.

Furstinger, Nancy. *Helper Robots*. Minneapolis:
Lerner Publications, 2015.

Kiddle: Robot Facts for Kids
https://kids.kiddle.co/Robot

NASA Science: Space Place
https://spaceplace.nasa.gov/space-robots/en/

Schaefer, Lola. *Human-Like Robots*. Minneapolis:
Lerner Publications, 2021.

Index

Photo Acknowledgments

Image credits: MikeDotta/Shutterstock.com, p. 2; Miriam Doerr Martin Frommherz/
Shutterstock.com, p. 4; Hero Images/Getty Images, p. 5; Professional Stock Works/
Shutterstock.com, p. 6; lzf/Shutterstock.com, p. 7; Ingo Wagner/DPA/AFP/Getty Images,
p. 8; David Cardinez/Shutterstock.com, p. 9; Monty Rakusen/Getty Images, p. 10; NASA,
p. 11; Roman Pyshchyk/Shutterstock.com, p. 12; Yullishi/Shutterstock.com, p. 13; elesi/
Shutterstock.com, p. 14; Valeriya Zankovych/Shutterstock.com, p. 15; MONOPOLY919/
Shutterstock.com, p. 16; Jenson/Shutterstock.com, p. 17; NASA/JPL-Caltech, p. 18; Master
Video/Shutterstock.com, p. 19; frenky362/Shutterstock.com, p. 23.

Cover image: Echo/Getty Images.